11 Tips to Investing in Real Estate

A Beginner's Guide to Real Estate and Avoiding Common Mistakes

Mike Hartley

Mike Hartley

© **Copyright 2023 - All rights reserved.**

The content of this book may not be reproduced, copied, or transmitted without explicit written permission from the author(s) or publisher. Doing so would constitute a breach of copyright law and could result in serious legal repercussions for any party participating in the illicit reproduction of the material. Furthermore, due to the nature of intellectual rights, it is impossible to duplicate or replace the original work produced by the author(s) or publisher; therefore, the only way to legally gain access to this content is through direct authorization from either party.

The publisher and the author(s) of this book shall not be held accountable in any way for any damages, reparations or financial losses that may arise because of the information contained herein, either directly or indirectly. This includes any potential harm, monetary loss, or other consequences from individuals' usage of said information. It is also understood that these individuals will not be able to use this clause to evade legal responsibility for their wrongdoings related to the content provided in this book. The publisher and author(s) will thus be free from all liabilities associated with the publication and distribution of this book.

Legal Notice:

This book is subject to copyright protection and should only be used for personal use. Furthermore, it should not be shared with any other individual or persons for any purpose other than that for which it was initially intended. It is strictly prohibited to amend, reproduce, distribute, utilize, quote, or paraphrase any part of the content within this publication without prior authorization from the writer or publisher. Any violation of these regulations may result in legal action against those who have breached them.

Mike Hartley

Disclaimer Notice:

The presented work is strictly informational and should not be interpreted as an offer to buy or sell any form of security, instrument, or investment vehicle. Furthermore, the information contained herein should not be taken as a legal, tax, accounting or investment recommendation given by the author(s) or any affiliated company, employees, or paid contributors. In other words, the information is presented without considering individual preferences for specific investments in terms of risk parameters. It is general information that does not account for a person's lifestyle and financial objectives. It is important to note that no tailored advice will be provided based on the given information.

The authors and their parent company, along with all employees and paid contributors, have agreed to abstain from trading any stock or investment written about for at least two days publication of any new article, book, report, or email. This includes any equity, options, debt, or other instruments related to that security, stock, or company, except for existing orders that pre-existed the submission; all such charges will be disclosed inside the document. The author(s) may have direct or indirect positions in some of the companies mentioned because of holdings in mutual funds, exchange-traded funds, closed-end funds, or other similar vehicles. Such indirect holdings are usually not disclosed as there is no guarantee that the author(s) is aware at any given time of the individual portfolios of any of these funds. Furthermore, certain decisions by these funds, such as buying or selling stocks, could potentially impact an author's position even if it was not done directly by them.

Warning:

There is no simple, easy way to become wealthy, especially regarding investments in the financial markets. While it may be possible to make a significant return on your investment, there is also a high risk of losing a large amount of money if you do not have the proper knowledge and knowledge base. You must conduct thorough research and analysis to succeed with investments with the most significant potential for price appreciation. Investing wisely requires an extensive level of education and an understanding of how markets work for one's portfolio to yield positive returns over time. Before venturing into any investment endeavor, it is essential to consult an experienced financial advisor or professional who can advise what steps should be taken and how much capital should be invested. It is also necessary to review all relevant information about potential investments, such as the company's financial statements and prospectus, to make an informed decision regarding whether to invest. Everyone must remember that past results are not necessarily indicative of future performance, so it is wise never to invest more money than you can afford to lose.

This work is based upon a thorough analysis of SEC filings, current news events, interviews, corporate press releases, and knowledge obtained through our experience as financial traders, investors, journalists, and educators. We encourage readers to be careful when making decisions involving their finances, as they are ultimately responsible for the outcomes of their choices. To ensure they have thoroughly informed themselves before making any investment decisions, we strongly advise readers to take the time to research each subject in more detail by seeking out additional sources such as third-party analysts or other reading materials on the web. Furthermore, we recommend conducting a comprehensive review of all available data to ensure each conclusion is well-rounded and sound by exploring multiple aspects of an issue or topic. Ultimately, we believe that a person's financial future will benefit from making prudent and informed decisions based on knowledge gathered from various sources.

Mike Hartley

The author(s) and any parent companies may be affiliated with certain investments offered. If any of these affiliate offers are made, it will be clearly stated, however, that such affiliation exists. It is worth noting that we do not, and would never, affiliate ourselves with companies that do not meet our high standards and ideals; we would not promote anything that we wouldn't consider ourselves, and in that vein, we aim to keep any affiliations with companies that we believe to be of considerable value to our readers, subscribers, and fans. We value your time and education and try our utmost only to offer the highest quality support.

All trademarks, whether registered or pending, are the property of their respective owners.

Foreword to the Series

Investing is a necessary and invaluable life skill that many people don't even realize they need. It allows you to create financial stability, accomplish your most ambitious goals, and secure your future. Whether it be providing for loved ones, avoiding the need to work past retirement age, or funding a dream vacation in Japan, investing requires a deep understanding of the principles of finance as well as those of self-discipline, patience, and sound judgement, free from any emotion or prejudice. While this may feel intimidating at first glance, investing can be extremely manageable with the right guidance and strategies that minimize risks while maximizing returns. By staying informed and educated on the basics of investing, we'll have you on the road to financial success.

Whilst this series masquerades as a comprehensive set of educational guides to the various inroads of investing, it is in fact a chronology of what I have learnt over the years - and from almost every aspect of investing there is. Growing up in a family that had relatively few financial resources, I was always driven to make something of myself and ensure the future security of my loved ones. One of the ways I set out to do this was by ambitiously aiming to make a million dollars in cold hard cash - which seems almost comical when I look back on it now as I had no idea why I chose this figure! A million dollars was just an arbitrary number that I decided upon when I didn't fully comprehend what it meant, or how life-changing it could be. I just thought to myself "I think having a sum of money would really help my family along", so, with this goal in mind, I began researching and investing in various different fields; from stocks to bonds to real estate to swing trading, and so on! My journey has been far from easy, but every step along the way has been incredibly rewarding as I've continued to learn about investing and building my wealth. Now, whilst making money is still a priority/hobby for me, having time with my family is what really matters - and is ultimately more satisfying than reaching any arbitrary figure.

Once I had achieved my goal of amassing a million dollars, it was not that such an amount was not enough; on the contrary, it is certainly a significant sum, and having so much money at once gave me a feeling of great accomplishment. However, I found that I didn't want to stop there. It wasn't just about wanting to make more money; it was about wanting to keep on experiencing the joy and sense of fulfilment from investing. As a youth, I had the dream of being rich and financially free, but with more experience, I now invest because I've learnt to love it! After sixteen years of engaging in this activity, I had finally come up with a system which enabled me to make consistent wins with most forms of investing. So, I figured, why should I let this newfound understanding go to waste? Why should I stop now when things were going so well?

When I decided to start learning about investing, I made sure that I was as prepared and organized as possible. I researched thoroughly, making notes on who offered the best services, the cheapest rates, and which brokerages had a reputation for being trustworthy. As someone who is naturally meticulous, it only made sense to take an in-depth approach to this as well. So, I made sticky notes, wrote in journals, and took copious notes in Word documents - all with the intention of compiling my thoughts throughout the process. Fast forward sixteen years later and here I am writing a series of books based on my experiences!

To ensure accuracy when writing this series from different perspectives - such as in 'Investing for Women' - I asked friends and fellow investors for their input to add further insight into each book. In fact, much of what is written regarding investing has been pre-written by me over time in various forms - be it a scribbled note or a more detailed outline of what I personally needed to know to invest in that field. Although not an expert in all areas of investment, through years of research and experience (and help from others!) I have been able to piece together content that reflects a diverse range of perspectives within this field.

Overall, this series of books is an amalgamation of much of my own research and experiences - some of which I have been continuing the entire time – others of which I've found either not profitable, or only mildly profitable, and so I've ditched them in favour of the better-earning ones! I have also included the thoughts, opinions and input from others involved in the investing world, to ensure accurate representation from a variety of perspectives. It has been a fun journey putting together all the pieces and rewarding at the same time. I am excited to share my knowledge and insight into investing with you all.

This series of handbooks provides a comprehensive guide for even the most beginner investor who is looking to start investing with confidence and ease. Each book dives deep into different aspects of investing, providing readers with the essential knowledge and information they need to make smart decisions when it comes to managing their money. These books are tailored specifically for those who want to gain a better understanding of investing in the financial markets and successfully managing their portfolios over time. Despite my American-based viewpoint, anyone can follow the principles explained within these pages regardless of their country. By reading this series from beginning to end, readers will be equipped with all the key tools necessary for success in investing and achieving long-term financial independence.

In addition to straightforward advice on how to invest, this series also offers guidance on everything from basic stock market terminology to more complex financial instruments. Readers will learn about diversification, risk management strategies, cost/benefit analysis, taxes related to investments, and more – giving them a strong foundation of knowledge that can be applied no matter what type of investment they choose.

My goal is for readers not only to understand what's going on in the markets but also to gain insight into why certain strategies have been useful for me, and how you can find the ones that suit you best.

Note:

I'm often asked what investments I'm presently making and it's an important question for those who are seeking to find financial freedom. After giving the matter a great deal of thought, I felt writing this information down in a book would quickly become outdated since I tend to rebalance my investments at least every three months. To provide readers with more up-to-date information, I decided to create a website which will help them understand what I am doing and encourage them to do the same. This website will not only provides details of the investments but also includes facts and figures that illustrate how these strategies can help people achieve their financial objectives. It will offer guidance on how to make wise investment choices and gives insight into the kinds of risk associated with each decision. Furthermore, this website contains detailed advice on how to maximize returns by diversifying your portfolio across multiple asset classes, mitigating losses through careful analysis of market trends, as well as other long-term strategies for achieving financial independence. By taking advantage of all the knowledge provided on this site, readers can feel confident that they have taken steps towards attaining their own financial freedom.

The journey to uncovering the secrets of successful investing can seem daunting, but I'm determined to make it easier for you! By subscribing to my email list, you'll stay up-to-date with the latest books in the series, and eventually be the first to know about my unique investment system. By being on the e-mail list I will also let you know when the website is launched too – exciting! I am constantly thinking "I wish I'd had this when I started! I'd have saved a decade worth of time!"

So, no matter your level of financial literacy, I have comprehensive information for anyone who is keen on learning more. With an array of resources at my disposal, I can give you an in-depth look at the foundation of successful investing. Through these materials, I will provide a thorough look into elements such as risk management principles and best practices, financial forecasting, budgeting techniques, and so much more.

On top of this knowledge base, subscribers will also be given access to exclusive tools such as calculators and other interactive features that can help simplify complex topics like portfolio construction. This way, no matter what your individual goals are when it comes to building wealth through investments - I'm here to help!

By joining my email list you'll have access to all these resources and more. So come on board for this exciting adventure and discover how you can get started investing for success today!

So, with no further ado, let's dive in!

Your Free Bonus Gifts

Accelerate Your Learning

Maximize Your Earning

We are here to help you crush it – no bones about it. To make the most of this book, there are two things you'll need:

1. **FREE RESOURCES**

   We have created a number of free resources for you to take advantage of. Use them to accelerate your learning and maximize your earning!

2. **FURTHER RESOURCES**

   We are constantly striving to continue supporting both our team and our students. We are busy creating a website to better highlight all of our investing tips, tricks and current holdings to help our users better see what we're actually up to! To find out when we launch this, and be alerted when we release other titles, just subscribe to our e-mail list and you'll be the first to know!

11 Tips to Invest in Real Estate

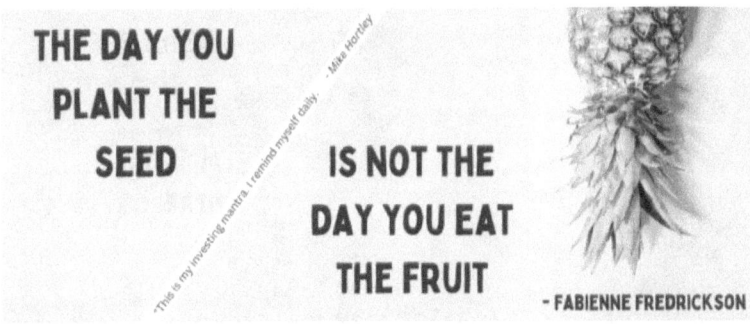

Subscribe To The Newsletter and Join Us!

- Find out the secrets to investing safely
- Join the growing **FIRE** (**F**inancially **I**ndependent **R**etire **E**arly) Movement!
- Live your passive income lifestyle…

www.thefirefund.com/free-gift

Table of Contents

Foreword to the Series _____ vii

Your Free Bonus Gifts _____ xiii

Introduction _____ 3

Chapter 1: Think Like a Landlord _____ 5

    Tip 1: Know Real Estate Investing Through Knowledge and Action _____ 6

    Tip 2: Set Specific Goals to Help You Take Action _____ 10

    Tip 3: Build Your Brand _____ 12

    Key Takeaways _____ 13

    Summary of Actionable Steps _____ 14

Chapter 2: Assess Your Capital _____ 15

    Tip 4: Assess and Grow Your Capital _____ 16

    Summary of Actionable Steps _____ 24

    Key takeaways _____ 24

Chapter 3: Chapter 3: Organize Your Assets _____ 26

    Tip 5: Building an Effective Network _____ 26

    Tip 6: Value Your Team Members _____ 29

    Tip 7: Paying Commission Will Increase Your Profit _____ 32

Tip 8: Find the Best Contractors 33

Summary of Actionable Steps 36

Key Takeaway 36

Chapter 4: Putting Everything on the Table 38

Tip 9: Pick the Best Deal 38

Tip 10: Know Your Key Performance Indicators (KPIs) 40

Tip 11: Documentation—Be Strategic and Train With Your Strategy 43

Summary of Actionable Steps 47

Key Takeaways 47

Conclusion 48

Bonus chapter! 51

Tip 12: Pick Consistent Marketing Strategies 51

Summary of Action Steps 55

Key Takeaways 56

Glossary 57

References 58

Introduction

Real estate cannot be lost or stolen, nor can it be carried away. It is purchased with common sense, paid for in full, and managed with reasonable care. Real estate is about the safest investment in the world.

–Franklin D. Roosevelt

Every human from all walks of life has goals, dreams, and aspirations. There are physical, psychological, health-wise, and, of course, financial goals that humans intend to attain at some point in life. Most times, the roadblock that restrains someone with these aspirations is a plan on how to make them come true.

Anyone can have dreams. You may fantasize about the fleet of cars you would love to have in your possession, the homes bought in your name, the expensive vacations, a secure retirement, and a trust fund for your children and grandchildren, amongst other financial goals. While these are valid dreams and you may, indeed, have a feasible plan to achieve them, the question is this: Are you sufficiently inspired to take the necessary actions? You should know that significant fortunes worldwide have been made via real estate. It is the quickest, safest, and most prudent way to become financially free. Unfortunately, like every other investment security, real estate is susceptible to risks. Do not fret, as the purpose of this book is to teach you proven strategies to exploit the real estate market without losing money.

This book will explore the various stages of real estate. More importantly, it will provide you with the necessary practical tips that will serve as a guide to prevent you from making common investing mistakes.

After reading this book, I hope to have provided a thorough compilation of reliable and helpful tips based on my long-term experience and affinity for all that has to do with investing. I firmly believe wealth accumulation can only be guaranteed through investment securities—real estate is the highlight. Nothing beats an individual who has taken their fair share of financial hits; after all, the wisdom that comes with experience isn't bought; it's earned!

> I firmly believe wealth accumulation can only be guaranteed through investment securities—real estate is the highlight.

This book is written with simplicity without compromising its comprehensiveness.

CHAPTER 1

Think Like a Landlord

I don't think poverty can be fixed without restoring housing, and I don't think housing can be addressed without understanding landlords.

–Matthew Desmond

When you think of investing in real estate, you imagine yourself as a homeowner or a landlord. One of the best ways to build wealth in real estate is to become a landlord. To execute actions that will yield fruitful results later, you have to think like you already have a home.

Real estate is ranked the most critical asset class over stocks and bonds by the total market cap. This chapter will cover vital tips on thinking and making good choices as a landlord. Foremost, you must understand what real estate investing is, the types, and how to set specific goals to kick-start your real estate investing journey.

Tip 1: Know Real Estate Investing Through Knowledge and Action

Every asset class in finance and investment requires knowledge and action to persist. You cannot afford to make impulsive or misguided decisions. Experts often advise that individual investors perform meticulous due diligence before putting their money into any investment.

What Is Real Estate Investing?

Real estate generally involves the purchase, sale, or rental and the overall management of real properties to generate profits. Unlike the dynamics of other investments, where they are traded via a market, real estate is unique. Its specific location determines its value. Aspiring real estate owners can make a partial payment of the total cost of the property in advance and pay the outstanding balance with interest.

Indeed, an excellent real estate investment with a high level of risk may have the potential to yield greater returns, but this isn't always a guarantee. The same logic applies to choosing a seemingly promising investment plan. There is still no guarantee that it will be as profitable as you have hoped.

Types of Real Estate Investing

Whether you are just getting started or have commenced your investing journey, it is crucial to know and understand the types of real estate investing there are to guide your choices. Since real estate investing can mean different things, some of the available options you can explore are:

- **Residential real estate**: This is the most popular type of real estate investment. Any property in real estate used for residential purposes, like apartments, condos, duplexes, and single- and multi-family houses, is usually active. That is, they require significant contributions that could either be monetary or in terms of labor to attain. Residential investments are prospective. If you find and purchase properties in the right area, they can be lucrative with a continuous cash flow. That being said, you must know that residential estate investments can be pretty expensive. For example, if you buy a house at a discount, you will need a significant amount of cash flow to renovate the property. It is crucial to weigh the pros and cons of residential real estate to decide whether it is favorable to you or not.

- **Commercial real estate**: Commercial real estate contrasts with residential real estate. The properties categorized under this type of investment are exclusively for business purposes, like offices, gas stations, hotels, restaurants, hospitals, theaters, stores, etc. They are also considered active investments because they require that you have possession of space and rent it out for business purposes. The inflow of cash is maintained when you receive payment for rent or decide to sell the property when it appreciates. If you opt for commercial real estate investment, your concerns may not only lie with the occupants. You'll also have to worry about its public appearance. Hence, the need to hire professionals to maintain a quality standard and manage other issues that may surface.

- **Rural land**: Land real estate refers to a raw property with absolutely nothing occupying it, such as buildings, pathways, or planted crops. It is an easy-to-acquire asset and has lower costs compared to other investments. Undeveloped lands are less expensive and cheaper to invest in, and they also appreciate over time whether you develop them or not. Often, investors rent their lands out to farmers who intend to cultivate and harvest crops or even rear livestock. Investments in raw land offer multiple choices at your disposal. You could buy and hold it until it appreciates, lease it out to farmers, or build on it.

- **Real Estate Investment Trusts (REITs)**: These corporations oversee several real estate investments in properties such as malls, offices, and hospitals. As an individual investor, you can consider REITs a passive investment, as you won't own the properties directly. Instead, you can generate income by investing in properties managed by a REITs company. REITs can come in handy if you are interested in a commercial real estate investment but have no capital to invest in any of the properties publicly listed by the company on the New York Stock Exchange Market.

- **Real estate crowdfunding**: This is a new dynamic in real estate in which investors convene on an online platform to pool their budgets and invest in properties that may have been impossible to fund as individuals. Like REITs, crowdfunding is a passive investment process that does not require large sums of money. You must know that while some crowdfunding platforms are open and available to all aspiring real estate investors, others may require that you show proof of a stipulated level of income before you are allowed to become a part of them. You can think of crowdfunding as a community that grants you access to unique opportunities without much hassle; the entire investment process can be performed online.

No matter your choice of real estate investment, each has profound benefits and considerable risk. Therefore, ensure that your investment choice aligns with your risk tolerance level.

> No matter your choice of real estate investment, each has profound benefits and considerable risk.

Start Getting Some Real Experience

Understanding real estate investing in all of its intricacies is vital and, of course, has its benefits and risks. Nonetheless, it would help to rid yourself of habits that stagnate your investment process. Some action in real-life experiences is all that you require to transition from being an investment rookie to becoming a successful professional. After all, experience, they say, is the best teacher.

Tip 2: Set Specific Goals to Help You Take Action

Everyone has personal and financial goals. You probably do too.

Are your goals simple enough to allow you to take the necessary actions to achieve them? For instance, if you aim to develop muscles on your thighs because they are very weak, do you ask yourself questions, for example, *How do I intend to achieve that? How many squats do you do in a week?*—among other questions that help you take the necessary actions? Individual financial goals are valid, but actionable plans are more effective.

Where You Want to Invest

Since you have specifically chosen real estate investments as your most preferred choice in a diversified portfolio, what type of real estate investment resonates with your bigger vision? Another criterion to consider when choosing is being realistic about your present financial capacity. Some types of real estate investments require a certain level of financial stability to get off the ground. You cannot invest in residential real estate if you do not have the funds to purchase or renovate buildings. Beginner investors with little or no capital are advised to engage in passively operated investments.

How You Want to Invest

A solid plan on how you want to invest in real estate can help you visualize a bigger picture of your short- or long-term goals and stay focused on achieving them. You may purchase a rental property if you have the capital to do so, and you may see your present home as an investment by buying it.

The latter has its benefit vested in the possibility of building equity from your monthly payments in contrast to paying rent annually. Who's to say that your annual rent won't rise over time? Ownership of your home guarantees that a portion of your monthly mortgage serves as your proceeds.

What Do You Want to Achieve from Investing?

Understanding what it takes to become a successful investor is one thing. Finding clarity in what you hope to achieve is another thing. Let's dive into the possible reasons you may have for choosing to invest in real estate, including its future benefits, for example:

1. Real estate investing helps build equity and accumulate wealth.

2. To meet your financial goals, such as stashing emergency funds, trust funds for your kids and grandchildren, and saving for college and retirement, among others.

3. To stay ahead of inflation.

4. To have a reliable and long-term source of income.

5. To attain flexibility and autonomy over your career as an investor.

Rome was not built in a day. Every life achievement is a process that requires patience, due diligence, and persistence to achieve.

Real estate investing requires the same procedure. Create a business plan that includes milestones for when you hope to achieve your goals, work towards them, and set a good reward aside for when you hit each milestone because you deserve it.

Tip 3: Build Your Brand

The essence of branding generally is to portray yourself to patrons as distinct from others in the same field. Branding in real estate differentiates your agency from the other options that home and commercial property buyers have. That is, it has to reflect a distinctive characteristic that informs buyers that you are a good fit for their unique requirements.

Core Value of a Brand

Your brand's core values are the unique beliefs you and your real estate investing company stand for. Think of these values as a map that guides what your brand goals are, how to achieve them, and the actions that surround your decision-making processes. Some of the core values of real estate investors are integrity, loyalty, honesty, commitment, accountability, and communication. Clients will only sustain relationships with brands that uphold these core values. Reflect profoundly and determine what your core values are. Then endeavor to emanate them, as they are what attracts prospective clients.

> Clients will only sustain relationships with brands that uphold these core values.

How Does a Brand Affect Your Profit?

The primary aim of your company should be to ensure that the services and products you offer customers are the peak value. At the same time, you can maintain a high level of appeal compared to your competitors in the market. Your brand is your identity. As such, if your core values change and you can no longer meet your customers' basic expectations, you will lose their trust and, ultimately, their commitment to patronizing your brand.

You must strive to uphold your brand's core values and effectively meet the customer's expectations to keep your profits up.

Key Takeaways

- Real estate embodies natural or artificial properties that include land, and anything temporarily or permanently built on it.

- Types of real estate investments include residential, commercial, land, REITs, and crowdfunding.

- Passive investments can be made through REITs and crowdfunding if your capital is minimal.

- Branding in real estate is an identity and a reflection of what makes you stand out from other agencies.

Summary of Actionable Steps

- You should take action and start getting the real estate investing experience instead of procrastinating.

- Create a draft of a specific investing timeline, including celebration points to ensure that you reward yourself for doing an excellent job.

- Write out a list of personal expectations and objectives you would love your brand to revolve around, find clarity, and take action to achieve them.

In the course of making a real property acquisition, the next chapter focuses on how you can evaluate and grow your capital to place yourself in a favorable position.

Chapter 2

Assess Your Capital

You cannot afford to live in potential for most of your life. At some point, you have to set loose the potential and take action.

–Eric Thomas

Capital, as an integral aspect of real estate investing, is required to purchase and invest in real properties and to manage both long- and short-term transactions. Whether you intend to invest directly or indirectly in real estate, you need an amount of capital or cash to begin and sustain the process. Sometimes, money and action are all you need to unleash your potential as a real estate investor.

> Sometimes, money and action are all you need to unleash your potential as a real estate investor.

This chapter will give you insight into the different methods that can help you evaluate and grow your capital to be substantial enough for investing.

Tip 4: Assess and Grow Your Capital

Real estate investors adopt many approaches to raising funds for projects. Experts opine that every investment that turns out to be successful has its foundation laid solidly on three things: its rental yield, the underlying demand, and, of course, the growth of its capital. To grow your wealth through real estate, you must become acquainted with the different approaches to assessing and increasing capital.

Private and Hard Money Lenders

Are you familiar with the terms "private money lenders" and "hard money lenders" in real estate? Investors may put it simply that a private money lender is an individual investor or a private organization that gives monetary loans without charging fees for points. Hard money lenders, on the other hand, are quite the opposite—they lend out funds to investors with charges attached.

Both money lending schemes have similar and distinguishing features of which you, as a borrower, may need to become aware. Hard money lenders are often asset-based. That is, they tend to use the value of real property to evaluate and determine the amount of loan to be given to an investor. You should note that because hard money lenders are usually corporations, they are organized, licensed, and more suitable because they have experience issuing loans to investors. They are also highly beneficial to new investors, and you can count on a hard money lending company to provide guidance and quick funding approvals. That being said, hard money loans attract very high interest rates, and as aforementioned, they require real property as collateral.

Private money lenders, on the flip side, are money-based loans. You are most likely to strike a deal with them on their terms. No criteria or policies guide the issuance of loans, nor does it require experience to operate. Private lenders can be family members, friends, privately owned businesses, or basically anyone who believes that your investments will generate returns in the future. Like hard money lenders, quick funding approval is guaranteed mainly because the system does not require guidelines or rules to approve the loan. You should note that because these loans are quickly approved and are usually based on the lender's terms, you might be required to pay them back within a shorter period. Also, the lenders might decide to hike the interest fees because of the 100% financing leverage benefit attached to it.

Self-Directed Accounts

Self-directed accounts are ideal for investors who want to exert control over their investments, save money, and generate higher proceeds. Here is how it works with self-brokerage accounts: You get the opportunity to select from every investment option in the finance world—from funds to individual stock investments. This way, you have absolute control over what you invest your money in and how you do it, compared to being subjected to a limited selection of investments based on what your financial advisor has laid out for you to purchase.

For example, if you open an online account with a discount broker, you have investment choices like the different kinds of funds, including whether you want to buy or sell individual bonds and stocks or dabble in other small-cap investments, etc. Not every investment account allows for this linear pathway feature in the financial market. A self-directed account gives you the precision that will enable you to focus on allocating your funds however you desire. One of the advantages of this method of assessing your capital is that it operates at a meager cost, whereas some other types offer a higher cost of managing mutual funds. Examples of self-directed accounts include individual retirement accounts (IRAs), 401(k) and 403(b) plans, and the ordinary brokerage account.

Private Placement Memorandums

The private placement memorandum is a legal document used by the owners of privately owned corporations to attract a group of outside investors. The document spells out the objectives, deal terms, and risks regarding an investment vehicle to understand it better.

As a form of investment assessment and in the course of performing your due diligence as an investor who intends to build a brand or invest in another privately owned corporation, a private placement memorandum can serve as a thorough business plan to generate the interest of your potential clients or to enlighten you as an investor on how the corporation operates financially.

For a better perspective, if you were to invest in a company, the following are the essential details that will be included in the offering memorandum:

- The company's financial statements.
- The terms of the investments.
- The nature of the business and its management's biography.
- The potential risks involved in the business.
- A subscription agreement (that shows the details of the contract between you, an investor, and the corporation).

The essence of the document is to prevent you (a buyer) from buying securities that are not registered. Also, from the standpoint of you building a brand, the document provides your clients with the necessary information to make a seamless purchase. It also helps you assess and eliminate the liability of selling unregistered investment securities.

Wholesaling

The term "wholesale" is familiar if you have been in the business world for a while now. If you have any considerations for wholesaling in real estate, you are looking to sign a contract on a property and sell it to another buyer for a commission.

It may gladden you to know that wholesaling requires no capital whatsoever. You can make profits off selling residential and commercial properties for a simple transaction fee that is usually a little above the actual price of the property without putting a dime on it. It is between the original seller of the property and you, the wholesaler—an intermediary whose job is to go in search of a buyer and ensure that the buyer meets the asking price of the property. For example, if a seller puts up a property for $185,000 to be sold within six days, you find a buyer (usually an investor or someone who wants to acquire the property for personal use; it could be residential) who is willing to pay about $190,000 within the stipulated time frame. Your profit is the difference between the actual price and the price you list it at

Wholesaling may seem tasty and lucrative, given that you can kick-start your real estate career without much hassle and learn more about how commercial real estate works while on the job. Nevertheless, it is essential to know that the buyer and the seller of the properties have a part to play in determining the margin of your profit. Over time, you may be subjected to generating a low-margin profit if you cannot find buyers willing to purchase at the asking price. Also, sometimes, sellers may be unmotivated to sell quickly or even uninterested in requiring the presence of a wholesaler to sell a property. This factor can make wholesaling an uncertain way to make a living. There is never a guarantee that if you find a motivated seller, a buyer will be willing to pay your asking price.

There are usually contracts binding sellers and wholesalers, and if you do not meet the requirements guiding the sale of the property, chances are that you will lose out on the profits. Wholesaling—like every other method of growing capital through healthy returns—has advantages and disadvantages. You must understand its process in an in-depth manner and weigh the factors carefully to determine your chances of doing well in the sector.

FHA Investment Loans

The federal housing administration (FHA), as an investment loan strategy, came to the limelight during an era when homeowners had extreme difficulty purchasing houses outright and maintaining payments via a mortgage. The terms were concise at the time, and homeowners were only limited to loans worth half of the property's value on the market. The United States Congress then proceeded to fix this inconvenience by creating the federal housing administration to enhance easy and affordable ownership of homes.

In recent times, statistics have shown that homeowners who are looking to apply for FHA investment loans are only required to have a credit score of 580 or above and make down payments whose percentages depend on their current credit score. This might not be an effective way to develop capital for your investments because the policies guiding the loan restrict investors from benefiting. Therefore, the only people it isn't limited to are those who intend to make the purchased homes their primary residences. You cannot qualify for the loan if you aim to finance an investment property, a second home, or a vacation house.

There is an exception to this rule that can help you generate rental income. It states that you can take an FHA loan to buy as much as a four-unit dwelling, but you must live in one of the units. The other three units can be rented out to generate income. By doing so, you can earn and develop capital to foster other investment processes.

Peer-To-Peer Loans

Peer-to-peer lending, also known as "P2P," is a form of obtaining loans directly from other people without the intervention of any financial institution. You may have been used to going to the bank when you needed a loan. With P2P, you can acquire loans without doing that through websites that offer this alternate method of financing. P2P lenders are the creators of terms and interest rates that affirm the transaction between them and the issuer. Most times, these terms are usually per the credit score of the issuer. Therefore, if your credit score is low, there might be a limit on how much you are granted. Also, the interest rates may be higher than those with good credit scores, who automatically have a lower rate.

If you have investment considerations for this method, you must know that the option usually requires higher interest rates to be safer. Most investors tend to assume the worst that could happen regarding potential risks. Then they ensure that the interest rates are higher. In the advent of any default, the interest rate will cover it. You can build capital via the peer-to-peer investment method by creating an account on any website that offers a loan and creating a platform for lending money to issuers. In most cases, these websites allow you to assess the profiles of these issuers to quickly tell who might have a high-risk potential and who would likely yield high proceeds via interest rates.

In some parts of the world, these lenders are known as loan apps. Generally, they are owned by public companies, which makes it easy for you as an investor to purchase their stock and become a shareholder who is entitled to a certain percentage.

Crowdfunding

It would help if you had a pre-existing idea of what it is to crowdfund for a cause, in layman's terms. People crowdfund for different reasons, often to attend to an emergency. Crowdfunding in real estate investing indicates that money can be raised for businesses via various social media channels to come in contact with an audience of conceivable investors.

It used to be a strategy devised by companies to raise capital during equity transactions to invest in the organization's future. As an investor, you don't need a lot to invest before you can kick-start a crowdfunding process in a relatively known corporation. The minimum amount to invest in a company is $1,000. Therefore, if the company eventually goes public and becomes well known, you will be open to the potential of generating enormous proceeds. While this is a valid standpoint, it would be an imbalance not to consider the adverse effect of crowdfunding. The question is, what if the company doesn't go public? Especially if it is a company with a very scant financial history, you could risk losing all your investments.

Therefore, it is advised that to avoid this financial drawback, you must do your due diligence by doing thorough research on the company before deciding to invest in it. This helps limit the chances of your investment not yielding excellent results in the near future.

Summary of Actionable Steps

There are diverse options for consideration in a bid to assess and build capital for other investment schemes. You should ascertain what method of capital assessment and development resonates with your objectives. Take a step and create the account, apply for the loans, or join the wholesaling team to find your bigger investing goals.

Key takeaways

- Real estate requires capital at some point, whether in the purchase of a home, in rent, or to buy land. You must assess your worth and understand what option best suits the situation.

- A private placement memorandum entails objectives, risks, terms, and a clear insight into a corporation's finances.

- FHA loans are created to offer loans to individuals who intend to make the purchased homes their primary residences.

- Peer-to-peer lending, as a financial technology process, allows people to issue loans via websites without the need to go to the bank; the websites set the terms and rates for the transactions.

- Crowdfunding offers individuals or corporations access to capital that would be almost impossible to raise independently.

The next chapter explains how your assets can be well organized and call on you to take the necessary steps to fulfill that purpose.

Chapter 3

Chapter 3: Organize Your Assets

In the business world, the rearview mirror is always clearer than the windshield.

–Warren Buffet

The real estate industry requires proper management and organization of assets to be effective. Tasks like monitoring and tracking assets, mitigating risks and navigating the complex legal and tax rules that guide real estate investment can be overwhelming. It should never be a one-person responsibility. The most successful companies did not reach their peak without an influential network of people.

This chapter expounds on the need to build an effective team and how to select the right business-minded people to aid in the achievement of your dreams of creating an efficient company structure. It also explores measures you can take to value your team members and how to identify each member's role.

Tip 5: Building an Effective Network

Building a real estate brand requires all the strategies and efforts it can get to become a huge success. The industry presents challenges that should not be underestimated. You will need all the professional and experienced hands you can find to build an effective network.

As soon as your business has finally reached the point where it requires the assemblage of a team, the first thing to do is to create a visual representation of your company's needs and the roles of the right people who will carry them out, including a structure for communication and business practices. The following are practical tips to make the process a little easier for you:

- Make plans and preparations in advance by evaluating what your current strengths are and realizing what goals have to be met.

- It would help if you did a self-assessment to affirm that you possess organizational and leadership skills to run a real estate team effectively. Most times, your team members are only there to support the growth of the company. You still have to take the lead.

- Ensure that real estate systems like business plans, objectives, goals, client databases, and referrals, among others, are well set in place.

- Determine what kind of team structure best suits your goals.

- Put effort into hiring the right person for the role.

You don't have to be saddled with the responsibility of building a network. You should not expect to do it all by yourself. Other investors who have scaled past this process and are now at the top never did it alone. It would help if you made considerations for people who could be formal business partners.

Tips to Find the Right Members for Your Network

The tips listed below will come in handy when you're ready to build lasting connections in real estate.

- Networking is about giving and taking. As such, you can connect with people by helping them in areas of your proficiency.

- Friends and family members who have a stake in the real estate market can be great additions to your network. If members of your inner circle have experience in buying and selling real estate, you should recruit them to join your network.

- You also want to meet with local real estate agents, especially those with a wealth of experience and skill. Such professionals provide you with expert knowledge about the area in which you want to invest. By attending workshops on real estate, you can meet with such individuals and gain other high-value contacts.

- Social media has proven itself, in today's world, to be a veritable platform for connecting with potential business partners, finding customers, and growing a highly profitable network. As a real estate investor looking to get the right contacts in your industry and specific location, consider using social media to achieve your goal.

Tip 6: Value Your Team Members

As soon as you have carefully selected team members best suited for the roles they have been appointed to, it is crucial to the growth of the business that they are held responsible for each role assigned to them. Hence, you should divide roles and be clear and concise about what is expected of each member. This helps to heighten accountability and efficiency by surrounding yourself with reliable and business-driven people who will be dedicated to closing more real estate deals for the company.

Having a responsible team means that its members can share knowledge and expertise, and they can also rely on each other to come through difficult situations that cannot be handled easily individually.

The Benefits of Valuing Your Team Members

As with any industry, the importance of valuing your team members cannot be overstated. Since these individuals are a part of your team because of their expertise, it's crucial that you show your appreciation for them regularly. You should accept their guidance when necessary and listen when they share their knowledge with you. This leadership attitude will foster trust within your team and promote better collaboration. As a consequence of valuing your team members, you'll set a healthy precedent for how they should treat each other.

Identifying Core Values and Responsibilities

It may be quite difficult to recognize the value that individuals contribute to your team without knowing your business's core values. It is only from this vantage point—a clear understanding of your company's core values—that you can assign roles to individual members of your team and give them responsibilities in line with the completion of specific objectives. Doing so will help you eliminate confusion within your team since everyone will be clear regarding their roles.

Establishing a Positive Work Environment

The last thing you want to do is allow distrust, fear, and negativity to fester within your team. One way to promote a positive work environment is by publicly appreciating your team, individually and as a group, for their effort. You also want to make sure that every team member is confident enough to share feedback with you, regardless of their rank or level of experience. This will enhance stronger bonds between the stakeholders in any project, and team members will feel respected and included.

Encouraging Innovation Through Rewards

If you want someone to repeat certain behaviors, one good approach is to reward the action every time it happens. This is called positive reinforcement, and it's a timeless technique to get someone or a group to act in the manner you prefer. If you hire competent and hardworking employees, as you should, chances are that you'll notice instances of creative input and innovation. To let these actions go unrecognized may drastically reduce their frequency of occurrence. Instead, you should always be observant and quickly reward what you consider positive behavior among your employees. This is an excellent way to motivate them to consistently strive for excellence, regardless of the difficulty of the tasks they've been assigned.

How Valuing Your Team Can Lead To Successful Real Estate Investments

If you've been in business for any length of time, you will notice that increased trust among project stakeholders often correlates with increased success. And as we discussed earlier, a good way to foster trust within your team is to show, in different ways, that you value your employees. You can achieve this, for instance, by training them, offering kind support throughout the lifecycle of any project, refraining from micromanaging them, and motivating them with rewards when they get something right. To build a successful real estate portfolio, your company culture should be one of reciprocal respect and appreciation. And this should extend to every stakeholder in the project, including management, every team member, and the clients. Such work environments tend to produce excellence and consistent profits.

> To build a successful real estate portfolio, your company culture should be one of reciprocal respect and appreciation.

Tip 7: Paying Commission Will Increase Your Profit

In running a real estate company, the bigger you grow, the more you will require agents to help sell your properties. When this happens, you must inspire their efforts by paying a commission. Securing productive team members and business partners ensures that profits keep rolling in. Therefore, you should know that these individuals do not work for you. Instead, emphasize that they work with you.

Since real estate agents are prohibited from receiving commissions directly from buyers and cannot work independently, you have to split the proceeds accordingly when the deal is closed, and the buyer makes the payment. Pay them the exact percentage that tops the initial selling price to foster trust and reliability between you, the broker, and the real estate agent. The annual earnings of a real estate agent are often determined by the number of deals they are able to close and the commission rate they bring into the company. It is important to note that there must be an agreement in the form of a contract that binds a property that will be put on the market by an agent. Commissions are always negotiable. They range between 5% and 6% of the selling price and should only be paid after a transaction ends.

For a better understanding, assume that you create a contract with an agent to put a house up at $200,000 for a commission rate of 6%. That is, the commission is $12,000. Perchance, if other individuals are involved in the sale of the house (like a listing agent), the commission has to be split between them according to the agreement. So, if it's 60:40, you keep $4,800 as the broker, while the agents keep $7,200 as their earnings.

Tip 8: Find the Best Contractors

The most effective way to create a rock-solid team of the best contractors is to rely on referrals. You may also approach reputable contractors who are currently working on or have finished projects in the same exact location as your building.

You can exchange contact information and indicate that you may have work available for them. Search for the company's name and check its profile online, including customer reviews, to assess it. The best contractors can be held accountable where and when necessary, and they have no difficulty adhering strictly to deadlines. They are also keen on instructions. Therefore, during the process of a walkthrough to assess a job done so far, if there is anything you see that needs to be commented on, you should do so.

In cases where you are unable to be physically present on the job site to oversee things yourself, do not hesitate to schedule Skype or FaceTime calls to keep track of events. With the best contractors, communication is everything.

How to Work With Contractors for House Flipping

House flipping is not a one-person job. It requires team efforts at every step of the way. It would be best if you had professionals who are well-trained to oversee the remodeling of residential and commercial properties and are capable of conducting rehabilitation.

In most cases, house flipping contractors provide all the labor materials, like engineering tools and other services necessary to facilitate the entire project. The need for general contractors for house flipping only arises when you are convinced that a property is beyond cosmetic and needs a good fix to put it up for an excellent market value. House flipping does not require work on the foundation; instead, it is more extensive toward the property's architecture.

For instance, if your project involves adding extra rooms, knocking down walls, or retrofitting, among others, you will likely need the expertise of a licensed contractor. To work effectively with them, look out for the ones whose specialty matches what your project requires. Do not be in a hurry to settle for one immediately. Make a small list of recommended general contractors and look over them once more to take your pick.

How to Pick the Team That Is Right for Investors

The following are actionable tips on what to look for when picking a team from the narrowed-down list that you have considered and jotted down over time:

1. First and foremost, run a quick check on the contractor's license to verify its validity. Usually, a licensing requirement includes years of experience and whether a written test has been formally taken.

2. Ensure that the general contractor is what you need on your team by assessing individual skills like carpentry, plumbing, electric work, etc. If they do not possess the necessary skills for your project, keep looking elsewhere; they are not the right ones for your team.

3. Insurance policies are essential. Make sure that the contractors are insured for a higher amount compared to the risk you are taking.

4. Look out for other qualifications like communication, professional, and organizational skills. Can they price a project accurately? Do they possess what it takes to foresee potential problems? Can they provide pictorial evidence of their previous projects to guarantee their efficiency? Can they quote reasonable timelines? These are questions to which you should find answers before making a decision.

5. Draft a contract to establish a trust system and a working relationship between your company and the contractors. Both parties must be committed to ensuring a successful project. Include penalties or bonuses where necessary.

6. Never pay upfront without a contract or an agreed-upon payment plan. Contractors who insist on being paid upfront without any paperwork set in place should be considered a red flag.

7. Important qualities like professionalism, the ability to reason, charges within your budget range, and, most

importantly, trustworthiness should not be sidelined or compromised. If you find a team that possesses these qualities, you are good to go.

Summary of Actionable Steps

- Create a plan of your goals and objectives and how you hope to achieve them.

- Build a strong network of professionals, and do not be scared to ask for help where you need it.

- Delegate responsibilities to team members accordingly and hold them responsible for them.

- Hand-pick carefully the best general contractors there are, be keen on referrals, and look out for reviews regarding the previous work done.

Build a strong network of professionals, and do not be scared to ask for help where you need it.

Key Takeaway

- Real estate is challenging. You will need knowledge, skills, networking, and persistence to achieve your goals.

- Organizing your assets requires that you seek the support of professional team members like agents and property managers, build relationships with business partners, and be able to negotiate contracts in ways that favor your company.

- Commissions usually depend on the initial agreement made by the broker and the real estate agent.

- Understand that you are not expected to do anything on your own. You will need to invest in finding active team members who will become part and parcel of your company's success story.

The next chapter gives insight into how to apply strategies, key performance indicators, and negotiation skills to pick the best deal for your company.

Chapter 4

Putting Everything on the Table

We don't have to be smarter than the rest; instead, we must be more disciplined.

–Warren Buffet

The practice of real estate is not limited to buying and selling real properties. It can be likened to a lifestyle—only that it can be the basis of independence and wealth. Therefore, when you lay all of your cards on the table, you must be strategic and disciplined in every course of action that you take next.

This chapter highlights indicators and strategic steps to evaluate when establishing a reliable real estate company.

Tip 9: Pick the Best Deal

Managing a real estate investment brand can warrant the need to find the correct answers to specific questions, but they are pretty standard. Even the most seamless course of action requires understanding and effort to yield desired results. It is one thing to have a plan for what you seek to achieve. It is another thing to fully grasp what it takes to pick the best deal for your brand's growth and success.

Buying a property is the most significant financial transaction most people will ever make, whether it is for residential or business purposes. There is a chance that you might make mistakes in the first purchase you make because you are not aware of certain pitfalls to picking a good deal.

These tips will help you choose a good real estate deal and save you hundreds and thousands of dollars from being wasted, for example:

- **Do not be in a hurry to make purchases and negotiate**: As soon as you have found a property to buy; you should not rush the process. Real estate deals sometimes come with pressure, and if you fall victim to it, you may have regrets. Take your time to assess the property and negotiate the price.

- **Consider the place and environment**: When investing in an excellent real estate deal, you must think long-term. Hence, the location of a property is essential. Is the environment vacant or overgrown? Is the economy growing and blooming? This, among other questions, demonstrates the circumstances regarding a deal and is important to evaluate.

- **Communication**: You must know that effective communication in real estate goes beyond your ability to convince a client to purchase a property. A successful real estate career is not a walk in the park. The digital age has made the process a lot easier through online marketing. Therefore, your interaction with clients and the impressions you make will go a long way in impacting your chances of picking a good deal. Master being an excellent listener to show genuine interest and strengthen trust. Your ability to reach your prospective client's emotions can go a long way.

Tip 10: Know Your Key Performance Indicators (KPIs)

Key performance indicators are employed to assess the performance of businesses and, in the context of this book, investments in the real estate industry. KPI as a metric fosters a more strategy-driven decision-making process through data. Industries that operate using KPIs usually have improved business outcomes because of their potential to give a clear insight into their business data.

In real estate, KPIs track more than just sales data. It is all-encompassing—from leasing properties to developing and managing them effectively. Whether you are an investor, a real estate developer, or an agent, key performance indicators are relevant in the field, and it's essential to know them.

> Whether you are an investor, a real estate developer, or an agent, key performance indicators are relevant in the field, and it's essential to know them.

The following are performance indicators you should know:

- **Returns on investment (ROI)**: If you are not new to investing processes, ROIs certainly will not be a new concept to you. No matter how little or big an investment is, a real estate investor wants to know how well the property will perform and what the profits are.

- **Net operating income**: A net operating income document accounts for how much money you make from a specific property. It indicates your total income subtracted from other expenses like taxes, capital expenditures, interest, etc.

- **Internal rate of return**: An IRR creates an estimate of the interest to be earned on every penny that you invest in a property. With an IRR, you get to understand a property's prospective growth rate, including an estimate of its proceeds on a long-term basis.

- **Gross rent multiplier**: A gross rent multiplier helps to compare potential and existing investments to deduce the property's worth. You must understand that the decisions you make regarding your assets should not be solely based on this indicator, as it does not account for other expenses.

- **Cash flow**: Cash flow as a metric is significant to every business owner and investor. It is an indicator of how well your business is performing. With cash flow, you can tell if you have been overspending or have made profits after subtracting your expenses; cash flow is the amount of net cash you have left in the end.

- **Tenant turnover:** Every successful real estate investor's goal is to minimize tenant turnover, that is, the proportion of tenants who retained a rental versus those that vacated. Tenant turnovers can reduce profitability, as investors must prepare a property for a new tenant when the previous one leaves it. Properties that are vacant for longer periods of time can result in losses of income.

- **Profitability per square foot:** This performance indicator is used by real estate developers to ensure that your projects will generate more profits through cash inflow.

- **Construction cost per square foot:** Certain requirements must be implemented with large-scale investments. For instance, you must understand how much space a construction will take and how much you will pay for that construction per foot. This way, you can quickly determine your budget for the project, including sale prices.

- **Real estate demand growth:** Demand growth as a performance indicator aids the easy forecasting of demand through appropriate aspects like population trends and mortgage application growth rates. This indicator drives the most successful projects.

Despite being measures that help turn your projects into financially healthy and thriving initiatives, KPIs are difficult to track. You will need all the supporting tools you can find to carry them out effectively. KPIs will aid investment decisions and help your team understand market conditions better, including how to influence and optimize costs.

Practice makes perfect, and you are not expected to achieve perfection at your first KPI application trial. You are encouraged to strive for improvements and consistently take steps that allow further progress.

Tip 11: Documentation—Be Strategic and Train With Your Strategy

In every successful business initiative, an official paper trail is an integral aspect. You need to keep track of every strategic plan and action; every milestone reached, and the details of every business transaction and evidence that serves as a record to reference in the future. Suffice it to say that the significance of documentation in real estate cannot be overemphasized. Ranging from records of the sale of a property to evidence of a change in property ownership, they can always serve as a traceable chain to verify the purchase.

> Suffice it to say that the significance of documentation in real estate cannot be overemphasized.

Depending on the type of transaction, some things must be

documented. A few of them are described below:

- Encumbrances are documents that place limits on the actions that can be taken on a property.

- An ownership list shows the individuals or companies to whom a property belongs.

- A lien priority says who gets paid first if someone owes money on the property.

- Mortgages refer to the various kinds of loans taken for the purchase of homes or lands.

- Estoppel prevents people from taking back what they had previously claimed was the truth.

- Foreclosures happen when someone defaults on their mortgage and the bank reclaim their house.

- Real estate fees refer to the money paid for the completion of certain real estate transactions.

- Real estate licenses validate an individual's or company's right to buy, sell, rent, or manage real estate within specific locations.

- Real estate deeds are documents that serve as proof of an individual's ownership of a piece of land.

- Real estate leases allow people, known as tenants, to rent properties for short-term use with specific rules set down by both parties involved in the lease agreement.

- Easements give people permission to use another person's private property for certain purposes, such as utility lines and roads, without actually owning it themselves.

How to Be Strategic and to Train With Your Strategy

Strategies and training as forms of assessment are critical factors to the success of any real estate or brokerage industry. New circumstances are bound to arise over time, and it's important to acknowledge the flexibility and make changes when and where necessary. The first thing to do is to set up a planning team that includes all the various types of departments for your brand.

Meanwhile, agents, investors, and other team members may come from diverse backgrounds and have contrasting previous experiences. You may realize that they might not possess specific essential skills like communicating and negotiating effectively and sales and marketing experiences, amongst others. Their former experiences might not align with what is required in real estate investing, but this does not necessarily have to be a deal-breaker. Therefore, there is a need to address all of these lapses and deficiencies through strategic planning and training.

The following are steps to guide you through strategic planning and the successful training of your team members to foster effectiveness:

1. A strategic plan for documentation should include an executive summary, a description of your company, a mission and vision statement, an industry analysis, goals

and objectives, your capacity, and, most importantly, a good marketing plan.

2. Ask questions like, "What is the present situation we have found ourselves in?" "What is to be done, and how do we do it?" "How can we create a link between our objectives and our capabilities?"

3. Teach core real estate skills like negotiation techniques, copywriting skills that can compel prospective clients to make purchases, and good presentation skills to show and entertain the properties.

4. Teach soft skills like active listening, picking up on social cues, practical communication skills, tactfulness, and, of course, patience.

5. Encourage team development through the setting of goals. You can also create an action plan that includes compensations when your team members are actively working towards developing their skills.

Note that sometimes, external facilitators of strategic planning may be more efficient than internal facilitators because they have no emotional investment whatsoever in the brand. They tend to be more logical about the process and ask challenging questions that have yet to be addressed. The essence of this dynamic is to create a healthy conversational platform for sharing ideas and opinions to make intelligent, progressive choices.

Summary of Actionable Steps

Create a list of essential factors to consider in picking a deal that best suits your goals and take small steps toward achieving them. Also, it would help if you understood your KPIs and their intrinsic value to the success of your projects. The better you know their value, the more likely you are to apply them. Documentation cannot be bypassed at any step of the way. Take strategic measures with your team members and external facilitators to achieve effectiveness.

Key Takeaways

- Consider location and environment when picking the best deal. Be tactful and do not make hasty decisions when negotiating the price of a property.

- KPIs are impactful when placed in the proper context. The process can be overwhelming, but it helps when you invest in efficient and cost-effective tools to keep track.

- Documentation in real estate entails creating a record showing property transactions to have a traceable chain for reference purposes.

Conclusion

Every person who invests in well-selected real estate in a thriving section of a prosperous community embraces the surest and safest strategy of becoming independent—for real estate is the base of wealth.

–Theodore Roosevelt

Real estate investing is a highly passionate pursuit that requires logical and intelligent actions, whether you like it or not, to achieve your financial goals and even more. When you consider the mood swings attached to being faced with highs and lows on the market, including older investors' minimal risk tolerance levels that may influence the direction the market takes through impulsive action, the consequences of these mistakes are inevitable.

So far, it can be said that this book has concisely explored eleven crucial tips to serve as a guide in avoiding common mistakes in real estate investing. Perfection is not expected of a beginner investor but can be attained through practice and consistency. As the common saying goes, "When in Rome, do as the Romans do." If you kick-start your journey as a real estate investor, you must embody the characteristics of a landlord—think as landlords do. This way, you can make intelligent strategic decisions based on the necessary knowledge. A landlord understands what real estate investing is, and he also understands the many types there are and which ones best align with his interests and goals.

> If you kick-start your journey as a real estate investor, you must embody the characteristics of a landlord—think as landlords do.

Having an in-depth understanding of investing is essential, but it is not sufficient unless you back it up with actions and efforts. Instead of absorbing chunks of information while *considering* how and when to implement them, you should get some real-life experience instead. Set a list of goals and objectives you would like to achieve, including the proper ways to achieve them. At every milestone you hit, you must learn to celebrate your wins—the essence is to motivate you to keep climbing the success ladder. As you climb higher, you become compelled to take more complex and elevating steps, like building a brand. Building a brand is no child's play. You must know what you want out of building the brand, where you intend to go, and what it will take to meet the demands of successfully running a brand.

This book further discusses the methods of assessing and growing your capital as a beginner investor, whether through wholesaling, investment loans, self-directed accounts, or crowdfunding, amongst other available strategies, you can choose. The advantages of building an effective network when developing a brand cannot be overemphasized. An individual cannot shoulder the responsibilities of building a brand and sustaining it; you need all the help you can get from business partners and team members to attain greater heights. You must know that this does not come easily either. Organizing your assets, valuing team members, finding the best contractors, and paying agents through commissions go a long way in building a successful brand.

One of the best ways to guarantee success in real estate investments is by being intentional about the deals you pick. Be sure to consider negotiation skills, location, the environment of the property, and communication skills, among other factors, when choosing a deal. Strategic documentation and measures like key performance indicators (KPIs) will serve as metrics to achieve perfection as long as you allow room for improvement and never stop trying. Do not hesitate to keep track of every milestone and cash flow for accountability and reference purposes.

> One of the best ways to guarantee success in real estate investments is by being intentional about the deals you pick.

Investing in real estate is one decision that will set you up for long-term financial freedom if you do your due diligence and implement these tips. You have made it this far, and it is only definitive that you secure your finances by taking this bull by the horns when you can.

Bonus chapter!

The aim of marketing is to know and understand the customer so well that the product or service provided fits him and sells itself.

–Peter F. Drucker

This book has ended, but you are in luck! I have included a bonus chapter with an extra tip to safeguard your investments.

Tip 12: Pick Consistent Marketing Strategies

Time and time again, the real estate industry will test many aspects, including how you manage your marketing. Knowing the right strategies to help you achieve your goals can take so much time. If you dabble in many options, you might spend quality time on the wrong approaches. No one wants to be in a position where efforts are made, but the results are poor—marketing costs a lot of money, let alone time.

That being said, a solid marketing strategy requires consistency to be fully effective, even after you have found the *appropriate* measures that best suit the services you provide. It is important to note that when you try out your preferred marketing strategy, you have to stick with it for as long as possible to guarantee that it is the best strategy for your business.

Some real estate marketing strategies that you can become consistent with include:

1. Know your audience. Depending on the aspect of real estate that you choose to become involved in, understand who your prospective buyers are to identify their habits, lifestyle, and needs. Finding a connection will help to build trust and ultimately devise ways to meet these needs.

2. Find partnerships and build a team. You should co-list with realtors, agents, and other brokers to survive on referrals to which you may not have access.

3. Hire a marketing team, as executing a plan will take time, and as a leader, you might not have enough time to shoulder that responsibility. It is okay if you are on a budget. You can hire a part-time virtual assistant.

4. Showcase your properties in good style. The vast majority of properties sold to clients were first seen as photos. These photos draw attention and stimulate their interest, creating a first impression of the property. If you put a property out on a social platform for sale, you might as well be creative by hiring an expert photographer, using drone shots, and taking your clients

on a virtual tour.

5. Get leads from your website. Aesthetics, though subjective, stimulate the average human's mind. Internet users can remain longer on websites if they seem appealing and can navigate easily through them. Therefore, design a compelling website user interface (UI) to make information easy to find, prompt clients to navigate and call you, and impress visitors with designs.

6. Adopt content marketing and SEO to provide relevant information. Maintain a valuable blog, publish free e-books, and improve your search ranking.

7. Use social media to reach your audience. Instagram and Pinterest are great websites to post your properties on. Moreover, since real estate customers often have questions regarding properties, you can use Quora as a platform to provide the answers. If your audience includes millennials, a great place to find these young investors is on Snapchat. Create amazing videos or kick-start a vlog series to market your properties.

8. When you build your brand, hire a professional designer to create a fitting logo to better indicate what your brand stands for.

9. Develop a stronger relationship with your current and prospective clients. Nothing appeals to clients better than a brand that emotionally connects with them outside of work. You can send postcards, care packages, or heartfelt notes to sustain a connection. You can also

ask them for referrals since 85% of prospective clients tend to trust recommendations from closer relatives and friends than distant ones.

10. Create a platform for real estate listings and reviews. Visitors can become compelled to patronize after seeing reviews from other satisfied clients.

Why Consistent Marketing Is a Must

Marketing is an integral aspect of building your brand to its peak capacity. Regardless of the kind of organization or business that you run, your brand is your most important possession—it reflects who you are and what you stand for. Therefore, you must be intentional about how your brand is portrayed, which directly impacts your current and future prospective clients.

Indeed, there are lots of contributing factors to the success of a brand, one of them being consistency in its marketing. Irrespective of the marketing strategy you choose, you must stick to a pattern or a schedule for implementing it. For example, if you run a vlog and only post one video per day, you must stick to that routine and not skip or be inconsistent. Doing this helps to build trust and credibility in your brand with your target audience, and you will also have a good reputation for reliability. You can utilize Google Analytics or Hubspot as a metric to monitor when your engagements are peaking.

Although it requires effort and hard work, being consistent with marketing does not have to be complex and arduous. Here are some tips you can follow to ease your process:

- Create a shared document that entails all your content ideas for reaching out and connecting with your audience.

- Ensure that each idea comes with a publishing schedule.

- Delegate due dates to each team member and request that one of them oversees the tasks.

While it is affirmed that maintaining consistency in a brand is challenging, you can be assured that it is a challenge you will be glad you took on—it always pays off in the long run. It opens the pathway to more business offers. Remember that in the absence of a regular strategy, you can confuse your customers. And as soon as confusion sets in their minds, your ability to establish credibility and build customer trust and interest will be difficult to guarantee. It would help if you made it all count when you could.

Summary of Action Steps

Emphasize quality over quantity by studying the numbers and documenting your strategies to improve consistency. If you have difficulty maintaining a firm grasp of your brand's statistics, it will be an extreme sport to map a plan that fixes your needs. Utilize social media platforms to market the services you offer. It will give a broader range of audience than those confined to your vicinity. Ask for referrals from your present customers and continue to solidify their trust in you.

Key Takeaways

- Consider online and in-person strategies to attract your preferred demographic.

- Marketing puts you out there to get noticed. It is an identity. It builds awareness just as much as it boosts sales—marketing is the growth baseline.

Glossary

Brand: This refers to an individual's or company's image, with which they can easily be identified.

Capital: This is an asset, often in cash form, that is the first investment in a business or used to purchase other assets.

Commission: This is a payment given to an agent (usually a certain percentage of the total income brought in by the agent).

Contractor: This is a company or an individual paid per project to provide a service. They may work independently or as a part of a larger firm.

Landlord: A person who owns a building or piece of land and rents it out.

Lender: This refers to a person or company that offers loans.

Marketing: This is all the processing involved in promoting products and services to attract customers.

Turnover: This refers to a business's inflow of money within a given period.

References

4 Ways to Maintain Brand Consistency Across Your Marketing. (2020, October 7). Mailchimp. https://mailchimp.com/resources/4-ways-to-maintain-brand-consistency/

20 famous real estate investing quotes. (n.d.). Realty Mogul. https://www.realtymogul.com/knowledge-center/article/20-famous-real-estate-investing-quotes

51 Real Estate Marketing Strategies: Ideas, Tools & Plans. (2018, October 2). Iovox. https://www.iovox.com/blog/real-estate-marketing

56 Eric Thomas quotes that will inspire you. (n.d.). EliteColumn. https://www.elitecolumn.com/eric-thomas-quotes/

Franklin D. Roosevelt quotes about property. (n.d.). AZ Quotes. https://www.azquotes.com/author/12604-Franklin_D_Roosevelt/tag/property

Hard Money vs Private Money Lender. (2021, October 16). NobleMortgage. https://noblemortgage.com/blog/hard-money-vs-private-money-lenders/

In the business world the rearview mirror is clearer than the windshield' - Warren Buffett; MHRenew American dream effort. (n.d.). EIN News. https://www.google.com/amp/s/www.einnews.com/amp/pr_news/596370465/in-the-business-world-the-rearview-mirror-is-clearer-than-windshield-warren-buffett-mhrenew-american-dream-effort

Mi, S. (2021, July 14). *Finding Contractors: Real Estate Investing.* Kiavi. https://www.kiavi.com/blog/find-and-work-with-contractors-to-flip-houses

Richardson, S. (2022, February 27). *Types Of Real Estate Investments: Everything You Need To Know. Rocketmortgage.* https://www.rocketmortgage.com/learn/types-of-real-estate-investment

Picklell, J. (2020). *A conversation with Matthew Desmond, author of evicted.* Apah Utah. https://apautah.org/a-conversation-with-matthew-desmond-author-of-evicted/#:~:text=I%20used%20to%20think%20eviction,inequality%20in%20the%20nation%20today.

Simpson, J. (2019, February 11). *Council Post: Why Content Consistency Is Key To Your Marketing Strategy*. Forbes.
https://www.forbes.com/sites/forbesagencycouncil/2019/02/11/why-content-consistency-is-key-to-your-marketing-strategy/?sh=734a6ce74ef5

Swaim, R. W. (2013). *Peter Drucker on sales and marketing*. PEX.
https://www.google.com/amp/s/www.processexcellencenetwork.com/innovation/columns/peter-drucker-on-sales-and-marketing/amp

Varun. (2022, May 25). *The Most Essential Real Estate Metrics & KPIs You Should Be Tracking*. Toucantoco.
https://www.toucantoco.com/en/blog/real-estate-kpis

Warren Buffett quotes about discipline. (n.d.). AZ Quotes.
https://www.azquotes.com/author/2136-Warren_Buffett/tag/discipline

www.ingramcontent.com/pod-product-compliance
Lightning Source LLC
Chambersburg PA
CBHW030453220526
45464CB00006B/2513